Let's Talk About
COMPLAINING

Distributed by:

Word, Incorporated
4800 W. Waco Drive
Waco, TX 76703

Let's Talk About

COMPLAINING

By JOY BERRY

Illustrated by John Costanza
Edited by Orly Kelly
Designed by Jill Losson

Living Skills Press
Fallbrook, California

Let's talk about COMPLAINING.

When people are not pleased with something and say so, they are COMPLAINING.

To COMPLAIN is to say that something is wrong. It is finding fault with something.

When you are around a person
who complains a lot —
- how do you feel?
- what do you think?
- what do you do?

When you are around a person who complains a lot —

- you may feel unhappy and disappointed;
- you may begin to think that the person is not fun to be with;
- you may decide that you do not want to be around the person.

It is important to treat other people the way you want to be treated.

If you do not want people to complain a lot around you, you must not complain a lot around them.

Too much complaining can bother the people around you. It can hurt you as well.

Too much complaining can make you feel badly. This is because complaining causes you to think about the bad instead of the good things around you.

Thinking about the bad things around you can put you into a bad mood.

When you are in a bad mood, you will be unhappy and most likely have a bad day.

You may also say or do things that would possibly hurt you or other people.

Thus, complaining can be harmful to you and to others.

This does not mean that you should not say anything when something is really wrong.

Once in a while it may be necessary for you to complain.

Think before you complain. Complain only if your complaint will help to change something that needs to be changed.

If things cannot be changed, accept them the way they are and do not complain.

When you must complain, do it kindly.
Try not to shout or to throw a tantrum.

When you complain, try to suggest things that could be done to solve the problem.

Once you are sure that your complaint is understood, listen to what the other person has to say.

If he or she shows you that your complaint is not fair, drop it.

If he or she suggests a good solution to the problem, follow it.

Try to think about the good instead of the bad things around you.

Enjoy and talk about them.

The less you complain, the more you and
the people around you will be happy
and enjoy life.